C000216410

Chance of a Storm

Rod Mengham's published poetry includes *Unsung: New and Selected Poems* (Salt, 2001), *Parleys and Skirmishes* (Ars Cameralis, 2007), *Bell Book* (Wide Range, 2012), *The Understory* (Corrupt Press, 2014), *Paris by Helen* (Oystercatcher, 2014) and with Marc Atkins a book of texts and film stills, *Still Moving* (Veer, 2014). He is also the publisher of Equipage, Reader in Modern English Literature at Cambridge University and Curator of Works of Art at Jesus College, Cambridge. He has published monographs and edited collections of essays on nineteenth- and twentieth-century fiction, violence and avant-garde art, the 1940s, and contemporary poetry. He has co-edited the anthologies *Altered State: The New Polish Poetry* (2003) and *Vanishing Points: New Modernist Poems* (2005). His translations include Andrzej Sosnowski's *Speedometry* (Contraband, 2014).

ROD MENGHAM

Chance of a Storm

CARCANET

First published in Great Britain in 2015 by
Carcanet Press Limited
Alliance House
Cross Street
Manchester M2 7AQ

www.carcanet.co.uk

We welcome your comments on our publications
Write to us at info@carcanet.co.uk

Copyright © Rod Mengham 2015

The right of Rod Mengham to be identified as the author of this work
has been asserted by him in accordance with the
Copyright, Designs and Patents Act of 1988
All rights reserved

A CIP catalogue record for this book is available from the British Library

ISBN 978 1 784100 83 4

The publisher acknowledges financial assistance from Arts Council England

Typeset by XL Publishing Services, Exmouth
Printed and bound in England by SRP Ltd, Exeter

Contents

After Archilochus

nothing is out of this world
or beyond the pale since Zeus
found night in the blue of days
left the sun at a nonplus
made men forever twitchy
now anything and everything
springs from the box
so what if the beasts of the field
leap in the sea like dolphins
the spouting waves are a charm to the ears
but not where the dolphins are
at rest in their mountain hideaway

Batavia

This portico was meant for the Sea Gate at Djakarta, but the eleven blocks of its arch and two Doric pillars never arrived, never came ashore. For most of the last 350 years they were loosely adjacent among the swells of the Indian Ocean. Now the shapes of individual column sections are all different. Flaws in the stone, areas of more or less hardness and resistance, open up and give way to pockets of memory, crypts for the imaginations of architect and mason. When their tools were laid out in the morning, they would pause before setting to work, close their eyes and conjure up a city, a forum teeming with men and music, the cries of shopkeepers, the chanting of processions, the baying of spectators in the amphitheatre. They would close their ears, but the gates were all shut, it was dark, the streets were hushed when the rain began, pattering in the dust, drops of blood from an unnamed cloud, in the lights and shadows of a different sky, where the circling stars follow old paths now forgotten.

It was a time to sow and a time for the radio signals to break up. The migrants would never return. The planes were all taxiing up and down the runway in a perfect *boustrophedon*. There were foraging parties disappearing into the hills, and in the middle distance a great plain where every citizen worked with a mattock, watched by the leader from a white pavilion. They would scratch a living in the time it takes for the songs of loss to change tune. All roads in the city led to that gate, but only one path led away from it, where streamwater ran through the grass and out among corals.

The gate did not know this, it would dream of another place, where the sound of bees comes down the chimney and the fields are prepared for dancing, where the crashing of waves is a distant lulling, and the patterns travelling over drifting sand are marbled, like the shadows cast from a great plane tree in the breeze of early spring.

With his last hand, the builder poured in the sea, and the ship sailed on to the studio wall. Beyond it was slaughter, the rescuers killing the rescued. Like the Shield of Achilles, the gate was forged

for enmity and rage, locked into place with the New Century,
in the rhythm of a march, of a pace-maker with armour plate.
The admirable shield is hung up or laid down, the immoveable
chockstone in an underwater gulley, perishing slowly like old soap,
cleansing nothing but itself in the empire of tides.

The Westralipede

Past the drowned roots of flooded gums, past the dead palm branches laid out like narwhal spikes, walking towards the coldest star in the southern sky when all virtue is exhaled, they are tearing up Newcastle Street in the next chapter of The Revolutionary History of Perth. Beneath the pavements other pavements. Or in Little Asia, Chinese clothes are on western mannequins and the Resistance Centre is closed, the Salvation Army is closed, the Rechabite Hall is closed, even the Daughters of Charity Bargain Box Closing Down Sale is closed. Three pleasure boats keep abreast on the lake, one of them rowed by two men with shaved heads and gold ear-rings. The man in the bows, image-spitting at the lake's surface, stares intently down into its depths, looking for evidence of the one-armed man last seen leaving the apartment. Three other men with brickbats wait under the flying buttresses of a Moreton Bay Fig tree, twisting the handles of their clubs. It is 6.00 pm, time for the first meeting of the Committee for Summer, convened by a bunch of peevish crows, wheezing like Mr Punch in a final attempt at a wolf-whistle. On this side of the tracks there are pre-paid funerals only, but I sit and listen to the eulogies on Dorothy Hewett 12 days after her death, watching a cortège of minuscule ants bear away the corpse of a black many-legged insect I do not know the name of. If I write less, I claim less against tax, while you pay more, although less for heat, light, etc. while reading this. Like the Amphisbaena, all texts here are double-headers: one to bite them that read, the other to sting him that writes.

Delivering the Device

For a second time in the fosse, beat back familiars, fare further. A necklace of villages, sequence of alternating loyalties, the double road-kill of rat and cat. On terraces of Grianan Ailigh, where winds blunder among granite briquettes and intercalated ferns.

Like a storm beach above waves in circling seas, the huge banks of rubble keep at bay allusions to the stealthy prow, chairs thrown over the cliff, a flight of Earls. One night, the sea was in the house. The currents were changing and men were dismayed. Now stones must prevail over time-sharing grass, tolerate thorns and thistles, giving a few yards of mesa.

Their daughters are cowled in a mesh of spider's web, a nearly invisible cloak over all the gougings-out. There are two revolving ringmarks on the one called Meg, burning asteroids that have many ages yet to travel.

These stones have been cast: limestone, granite, red sandstone— red sandstone in all the garden walls here encrusted with ballads. Two girls were found on the sunned pastures of the north east. The standing army forms up sporting blue jumpers and black straps in polychrome columns, your mission should you choose to end it.

Terra Infirma

The lights get carried away in this journey to the burying-ground
by the harbour, where a necrotising linctus covers the eye. Off to
the right, Seurat's bathers are gradually de-pixellated. To the left is
a seething weir. Beyond the vanishing point, under reflecting oil,
the dithering stems of angler fish begin to shine.

In a closed wing of the gallery are the specialists in mis-colouration,
the architect of the Blue Wolf and the Master of Female Half-
Lengths, whose ruined torsos break the surface of the painting like
foundation stones in the shallows, frost burning the extremities
night after night.

To pass through the looking-glass either to lose time or to gain
time is to change places with a detective dusting for finger-prints
between mirror and mercury.

Acting the part for which he became famous much later, the artist
secured his image in a dying cascade of photons by packing the
abyss with an infill of carbonised grain. They performed the arrest
when a lost masterpiece began to ooze from the stones of the
arcade. The memory of its pigment was a balm and a comfort.

The creatures of the deep are everywhere except straight ahead,
hyphens bringing darkness to its destination, soured by invisible
rains.

I took the first watch, knowing that nothing would flower until
the thought of a single tail-feather should slow down the rate of
decay. It is not known for certain when the mists began to form.
An end to this coshery.

9/11 is the date when the CIA-funded coup removed the Allende government from power in Chile

The hideous bunker of the military academy, belted with lawns and groves for contemplation. A single soldier in combat fatigues on patrol as if hunting for cigarette butts along the perimeter fence. The trees in the avenues outside look like olives but are relatives of the northern ash. At the junction of Avenida Amerigo Vespucci and Avenida Presidente Kennedy is a pre-Columbian statue on a traffic island, massively hewn like an Easter Island figure, its blank eyes peering at endless gyrations of traffic, backed by a wall of nicely interlocking granite blocks, and compèred by gashes of pebbles in the irrigated golf-course turf. At the same hour every morning, pariah dogs gather in a baker's dozen to parley and skirmish.

The chimney cowls nearby all have metal vanes upon their crests. Silently and in formation they swing round. From deep within the foliage of the largest chestnut tree a bat-like form depends.

Pablo Neruda, pinching lemon balm and rosemary on the terrace of his house, watches the column of soldiers climbing nearer. Diplomat, double, pseudonymous poet, furtive lover, collector of marine bric-a-brac, architect of the uninhabitable, guardian of the unruly spring, cultivator of profiles, prize-fighter, mourner, scourge of the peaked caps and the riding boots, founder of a sleeping tradition, he imagines the order in which they will destroy his works of art. Juanita floods my thoughts is the graffito on the stadium wall.

As far as eyes may see, there is spectral smoke on the runway to the east; in the west, the ghost-ships of the clipper trade, skippered by mutineers, coasting endlessly, silently at first, running the course debited in all the accounts, until the time laps itself, winning and losing, the wind stops dead, a centre of appeasement, the sea is beating its gong.

Lady with Vermin

Light on hands and cheek-bones. The hands of M, of a concert pianist ready to grip and force the life out of any being that strays into the killing zone. The hand that holds the pen or brush, conducts, fights and crushes lice and fleas.

These infest the hair helmeting the sides of the head, cross the neck encircled with a noose of alternatives, two ropes of beads, one falling over the breast, the other drawn tightly round the gorge.

Mind over vermin. The pointed chin of a brain-holder, switching attention, meaning only one thing at a time. The body stiff and alert while two fingers stroke the vicious accomplice, reaching slowly into its animal fascism, re-phrasing a dangerous habit, re-building attachment to a bow-string.

The insect skull of Peter Lorre, plot-combiner, image-magnet, constantly moving vehicle of race neurosis, the migrant who survives by performing the menace he fears most. The severed limb reacts to heat and cold, the nerve-centres project a gauze of lethal memory, a studio mock-up of Silesian pit-heads, clinker-built viaducts, sand in the fields, street violence flowing from one township to the next.

The hand is a graft, a spare-parts transfer, pulling the trigger of annunciation, distilling the national grid, with a crackle of energy that jump-starts the blood plasma, in a cloudless sky. The current surges in the exile's letter, in fractious demotic, bristles for a moment in the sub-surface brushwork of a salted-away predella. It is leaching out of the building, reversing away from the synapse, rippling through the flattened scales in the lizard serenades of Paolo Uccello. Keyboard nose-picker, opposable mouse-trap, angelic cattle-prod.

A Promethean gust of red pigment is blown through fingers onto the wall. A shadow-play of Cappadocian earth. The stencil at source, lithic photograph. The hands of realism are parasites of the brain, smell-feasts, mouth-friends, mess-mates at the sacrifice, repaying the landlord with flattery. Minor oscillations will gradually cover the ground bass of a vibrating string. In the interests of fuel economy, the guests eventually kill their host, savaged by his own lap-dog, first and last suitor in the art of house-training. This was an occupied zone, a hyphenated culture, the quality of the parasite determined by that of the nearest accented vowel.

Five Year Plan in Four Years

The narrative begins with expulsion, the shunning of sympathisers, secret informers, a belief in connivance. A single police car in the sun, parked up with open door, the afternoon cigarette, the endless fields, creeping stubble fire.

Dressed in a white coat, she walks out into the storm, past moss-grown piles of rubble, stacks of old girders and dead brush-wood piled up over many seasons. A drainage ditch clogged with reeds runs behind the houses and across dirt yards without a single blade of grass. Mature silver birches with charcoal-coloured bases are scarfed with dead grey leaves. On the outskirts, she reaches long low buildings with overhanging eaves and countless loading bays.

In the middle of the forest there is a tennis court of beaten earth with two deeply etched footprints on its verge. Nearby is an abandoned roller with weeds growing through its fellies. Further and further away from the houses along the forest paths as they get smaller and smaller, she finds orchids, ragged robin and death's-head mushrooms.

The deep, muffled explosions become clearer, the dogs are raging. Beneath the strains of an unaccompanied lament, the distant voice now seems to be that of a commentator at a school sports day.

The old cemetery wall has been gutted and rebuilt with a patchwork of stones and bricks and blocked-up doorways. Early morning drinkers shift from foot to foot on nearby waste ground, clinging to night-time memories that no longer fit. A plastic football bangs onto the synagogue wall beside them, routing a gang of pigeons bathing in a dirty puddle in the shade of a lorry. The one chic café uses the tables, complete with sewing machines, from a basement sweatshop long since robbed of its workforce.

In the middle of the Plac Nowy, a young motorcyclist dismounts, wearing the crafted simulacrum of a German helmet, and waves a greeting. The graffito behind him proclaims 'Skin Heads', the atrocities kept alive and rejuvenated through the medium of English. A vile flood covers the sealed well-head, the exact combination of pollutants having changed since the time, sixty years earlier, she had dropped dead in a street in Radom.

These days the only people who work in basements stand in artificial light all day, directing people into toilets. At Olkusz, the railway station now has no exit from the booking hall to the platforms, and no entrance to the passenger foot-bridge. The gate is welded shut, but a path has been trodden past the end of the fence, over the railway lines and onto the end of platform two. The orphanage dormitory is filled with sudden movements suddenly stilled.

The system of repulsions begins to overheat, realigning the currents of patronage and influence, erasing the last thread-like connections to the dream of a total environment. The urban planners simply reverse the flow of traffic, rewind the training videos, encourage the transhumance of memory and increase the number of request stops, blaming compass error and deviationism when the older drivers set off on a mystery tour. They endure a moment of stabbing pain as they re-join the motorcade, walk down felted corridors, breathe aimlessly their pocket of air.

Suffixes

I am addressing the female everyman of Saffron Walden
who is stiffening the lover's resolve in Bishop's Stortford

your voice an idiotic fanfare
your eyes saying we never die
and your single numb limb with its false rigours
and funny little teachings
                       like a giant thought or inference
cooking in the microwave

lashed to this estrangement and half in love
I cannot give a name to these red and raw striations
to this dripping wing of blue feathers

if all they are saying percolates down
and the corals of your mind drop away from memory
a majority of accidents occur in
conjugating Latin, during electrical storms

or during electrical repairs
birds fidgeting among branches
die here and now in the ditch
every one in its epoch
and stars shoot over
                    without breaking
the amorous mist
                along the milecastles

reader, we await your vice-hard grip,
your lassoing refinement
                    and your credit rating

the hidden ice presses one body against another
to confound the gathering wave
                      running back into the flood

I shall eat my leek plain
with two fingers of gargle
to effect a mountainous repose
before striking camp
                    in this wide gulf

where the moon has been flying solo

and arse-fingering dawn
                    has taken me in
again

Bend the Bow

no stopping thought it begins to sting

ministers deny rendition
rivers flow backward to source
I feel them glide

I had better jump in to scrape the keel
with a handful of red sand

the sixth of April, one o'clock
you undergo an obscure rite
to call the dear ghost back
otherwise lost
                the flower grows old and recondite
your face has ineptitude
                    and lizard crevices
written all over it

the lack of a truce has always gnawed
at Torchy the Battery Boy
all senses under contract
                to wring it out of him

oh, happy wandering mind
changed to a voice

send us some black snow

I know the way to cheat myself
                without redress
nor Rother, Arun, Adur, Ouse
                nor mind erased

Bust me! the stillness
frequent like the tide
like apples that fall by night

the snow alights on the windlass
the waves work less and less,
give place to glass

soft boys and fearless girls
hold on to your doubts

a horn blows from the fire and the rain

so fold this page and tear

The Debauchery of Nuances

The psyche puts on weight splendid and vulgar beast
it must be replaced by swansong. We throw out its rotten
awkward freedom of grammatical whirling objects.
They are the customs and excise values of too few bodies
the rest surrender all dignity like paint
running over the fabric of scraps of canvas
called painting. Hysterical creatures called
while you were out. These are their lips on the laurel
leaves with which we screen the cowardice of
ecstasy aesthetics, instead of actually the muzzle
the mouth we are pulling down at the corners
the mask of pornography. The shortest words and the
longest have been dead for some time. Their slaughter
is hygienic with linen provided, the voices
will seem more enchanting. Rubbish pavement sculptures
serve as spice towards everything we breathe
crushed with insufficient atmosphere:
a nightingale we can fold up flat
in an incomprehensible mumbling primitivism.

Engineering Works

How they brought the good news
will count for nothing beside
the infill of words in your mouth
forensic evidence of pentameter
travelling across space. OK, listen
the post-it note was for your eyes only.
I need this like I need a sense of viduity
or the death of bees in the hive.
The beginning of the end of the queue is the fourth estate
bored to death with its own freedom. Is this prosodic enough?
A flotilla of sighs and naufractuous groans
rally to the standard and demand a plebiscite.
Do not attempt this in a tremulous voice
the thing for taking stones out of horses' hooves
is broken in two or is lying asleep

in the long file of the wood cutter's enigmas.

Ad Nauseam

You could not remember our tune you prefer a medley
on the castanets. Your whole being was telling me
I have no choice. One hand on the tiller the other letting go.
The tiller gives nothing in return
only a splinter in the quick of the nail.
This is a hard lesson whatever it costs
conjuring thought from the poem before last
even to speak is to struggle.
Between bystanding and sleepwalking is a fine line
and I don't have the nerve to ask.
Would she steal away one Lapland evening
before the backsliding dawn. You strike while the iron
is conveniently arranged. I stoop to pick up things
in your path where the dust gets.
But you suspect nothing and travelling blood
has its own indifference. Shoot anything that moves or carols.

I speak as I find and this is the emergency reading room.

Repeat This

You have lost it was my fault but there's more
I live close to the tramlines the phrases heat up.
Too late in the journey a torch endues me with

shadows I have made up nothing all day
nothing has been changed
choosing between ferry ports at the last moment

not to mention this tonguing
which takes the bit between the teeth.
I am just going to put my head round the door

nothing like a change of thrills. There could be no doubt
this part was played by a separate instrument.
I await my turn which approaches fast

that's what life used to be like
kneeling down to receive everything
in the first few seconds. Asleep under the horse chestnut

it is always a question of layers
there is a ravine I am waving
all at once you retract your claws

where the blood has turned. I love you systematically
but time is against me
write everything you know I am not coming back

Coal Train Still Life

When you want language to understand
It bangs on all the doors, insulted by its own echo.

It gives you a lesson in longing. It walks out of the sea
Like a form of pure registration.

Dying each word goes where no other follows
Dying others come and take their place.

At the base of each forest trunk the whole world wavers
A small part of my body has lost its elasticity.

Take care how you layer the nest
It is time for my nap in the cradle of gravity.

Coal train, still life, join them up
Between grieving and forgetting that work in the same lab.

It is as if spring leans its head on your shoulder
As you cross from one time zone to the next.

The dawn is all washed up
It chokes the plough as clear as mud.

Horses' hooves rise out of the steppe.
I sing all the signs that come to your lips.

At the Furthest Point From Land

He woke up one morning a poet

too soon I tear it up again and find
the poem in retreat; with a scuffle in the ranks
of the most defensible sounds. It is not a dream
the simultaneous sorrow and attempt on my life
that is a poem. You have signed the order of execution
it still has your breath on it. There is no mistake:
the poems have engorged the lives of everyone we
tried to love.
     A subscription has been raised
to deprave and corrupt traditional methods of
reading without inhaling; and the one and only homology
has the right to ask whatever it wants.

Icebergs patrolling the North Atlantic
show they have nothing up their sleeves;
with each pang of an iceberg's heart
the flowers open and close

and I do little more. But this
bridging of the gap between the eyes
flies in the face of ears, nose and throat.
This clod of beef is my double.

At the news of his death
for which I have saved up all my grief
I decide to give him what he wants.

The Voice Left Me the Opening and Closing Word

When theory puts on flesh we discuss Hugh MacDiarmid
And how most of the doors have been forced

Then I fall into the arms
Of this body in the abstract
Her hands good to touch

From time to time I follow the movements of the harbour-tug
Back at the beginning I lost my way

So I retrace my steps, go over and over
Whether I have spoken this or two or three others

With the war-guilt upon us
We have enemies in common

We even share the physical tic
Melting by day and hardening by night

No longer longing for anything much
Only the livid overflow of dream

And the shadow behind us the immense wingspan
Of time and the waste of time

Enclosed within its eye is I

With a start we begin to fall asleep
To the sounds of the discontinued

And I feel just like an Armenian among you
Lighting my flares in a closing world

Icarus Alight

He is a diver to the inky cold of the ocean floor, among blind
crabs. Volcanic tapers flare briefly. Cormorant fledging breaks
away from gelid wax. Oiled skin breathes the Kleinian blue.
But pressure rattles the lens, changes the convexity of the eye.
Microbes in blood are projected as giant single cells, grazing on
beds of coral. Currents of lymph sweep away the pin-head sharks
and invisible squid. Retinal flurry translates into rushing shoals
leading him down to muffled chasms, cathedral rocks. Breathing
equipment shuts off, oxygen tubes flatten, general failure of
instruments measuring depth, pressure, and the malignity of the
earth's crust.

The image reservoir begins to leak, its sides buckle and a stream of
lost memories is released, patinating the shell-sand, touching and
electroplating the barbels of stretchable deep-sea fish, tinsellating
the legs and feathers of tightly packed barnacles. The memory
particles attach to everything, like revolving crystals they collect
on drowned machinery with its shuddering variants of systole and
diastole that stir the oceans into far-off convulsions. Glowing on
the soft obscure sediments of the deepest trench are minerals of
the dead and dying utopias of the spirit, decomposing evidence of
the crimes committed against them.

The diver falls to earth, impelled by a need to inhale information
in its purest form, through bones in the ear, finger pads, nerves
in the tongue. The small red coral branch hanging from a chain
round his neck looks like a miniature version of the pulmonary
tree. Gills close up as he breaks the surface, lunges into a thick
atmosphere, an ever-replenished gruel of toxins, bright mucus
lining the receptors, gravity installed at the prime meridian, lead
boots sucking a mud path on the Greenwich foreshore.

He ignores the Ravensbourne, Earl's Sluice, even the Neckinger,
with its outlet at Shad Thames, Venice of drains, making for
the Effra, sewage outflow for MI6, slurry of broken codes,
expelled communiqués, abandoned Cold War semiotics, attack
timetables, arrivals and departures all reversed, the current

switching backwards every time an agent is turned, the birth of deconstruction.

There is a short gap of attention, a hole in time, spent hallucinating the schematics of a missile guidance system, then a reversion to London clay, brick-earth, peat. Less than fifty yards away, the stumps of the bronze age bridge, the first boardwalk, angle towards the lost island of slippery gravel, dropping-off point for votive telegraphs, failed intercepts, entire lives engaged in passive sonar finally switching to active, hearing nothing, no echoes, no target arousal.

Crossing to the other bank he enters the Tyburn channel, passing upstream via underground cutaways to the Fleet and across to Hackney Brook. But he takes a wrong turning under the Holloway Road, rising through a storm drain in Canonbury, eyes on a level with spinning wheels, subliminal war-damage, the promethean slumbers of the homeless. On the Ball's Pond Road are babies given fried food in polystyrene cartons. Then St Paul's Road, with its dead window boxes, crumbling plaster acanthus leaves and hurrying felons, almshouses and £3 haircuts. The traffic resembles a bus-driver's funeral, so he crosses the road, sensing the hydraulic derangement of the New River, with its back-pumping system, and opts for a small, dark pond lined with teazles.

He is beginning to feel traction on the respiratory zone, gravity unwinding the lungs, shrinking capacity, hurrying past Canary Wharf and onto the Isle of Dogs, searching for a ditch in which to lie down and monitor the tidal volume, remote sensing the energy transfer between glucose and the liabilities market, bonus-mongering behind open doors and poetry's frozen assets, closed tanks, oxygen inertia, the perished mouthpiece, the rusted valve. Between the concrete ramps of the Silvertown road system is a triangle of grass with a broken bale of hay and an old bath to collect water. At a racing trot, a black horse comes flying out of Tidal Basin Road and carries him in its slipstream.

Then the patella on the left knee stops working as the brain delivers an enhanced nerve supply to webbing between toes and fingers, gearing up for the return to sender, as he limps off to scout

the Essex coast for a suitable thicket of reeds, a shelter, until it is
time to slip away unnoticed, last seen hurrying to the Naze, skin
now itching and stinging, eyelids malfunctioning, when suddenly
the weight falls away from the balls of his feet and exhales from
his shoulders, readying for a change of scales, the underwater gram
outweighing the kilogram of air, no longer confused, blocking out
tidal creeks, the entangling currents, a heap of coal, wreck-wood,
willows and osiers, encrusted bottles, the oystercatcher runways,
lugworm retreats, drowned pinions, breakwater slime, gull
squawk, crab debris, an entire hoard.

Five Portraits

for John Gibbons

1

Underneath, where the atmosphere grows up, grows old, thickens
and thins, and the space is tightly wadded, layers of air folded
and pressed, taking the weight, the burden. Inside, where a vessel
holds the taint of forgotten light, like a film about to be rewound,
removed, or projected into a future already past. A reliquary of
that future, turning on the spindle of memory, worn away by
touching and re-fleshed in the armourer's house, jointed and
blistered and splinted, the ball-hammer's duet with tenderness, the
acetylene caress. Waiting an entire life for the door to come ajar,
this door there, the one intended for nobody else.

2

The rotating shaft that funnels sounds of the night: the light
stirring of a child asleep, a latchkey unsettling the dark, the
reluctant breathing on the stair. A century passes. The late rising
of the hotel guest, the jailhouse conversion, cellblock showroom,
the aesthetics of high windows, disciplinary sundials. Nothing
can still the traffic of images, or the call in the street from another
time. We lean out to look in both directions but nothing turns to
meet our brief excitement, or long-lost speculation. Somewhere,
someone we forgot long ago beds down in the entrance to a
tunnel, and the floodwaters begin their advance.

There are thirteen ways of looking at a white blackbird. One is to place it on the edge of your belief system, it changes colour as it flies from one world into the next. Another is to tease it onto the margins of a sacred text, but perhaps this way is the same as the first. A third method is to hunt through the wood from start to finish, always two seconds away from actually seeing the bird. A fourth is to walk backwards through the wood guided only by its song. The fifth way is the way of impatience, the pot calling itself white, and the kettle calling itself black, until both are blue in the face. The sixth way is nothing like the third way, although rumours of famous success rates have been circulating in County Clare. The seventh way is to discount all reports coming in from County Clare. The eighth way is an adaptation of the twelfth way and is therefore always inscrutable. The eighth way and the ninth way cancel one another out. There are ten green bottles hanging on the wall, but don't get me started. There are eleven good reasons for abandoning a prose poem entitled Thirteen Ways of Looking at a White Blackbird. Twelve are the ways of Oisin, the wanderings of Aengus, and the heavy blows of Finn; the blackbird was sacred to all three, although far from being white, and never even a doubtful grey. The thirteenth way is the way of patience, and the only clue into the maze; this nest of words has taken many seasons to get right, but is not favoured by migrants. White Blackbird wins by a head, Throwaway comes second, in third place is Alfred de Musset, while the last flight into Knock airport is christened Grandfather Always Knew Best.

4

From here you can see onto Inishmore, the barley growing short by the sea's edge where swallows ride the tremors of hot air. The fretful tides below await their turn, and the birds in relay swoop to the sea but never touch it. Gulls watch the retreat of a small black dog with a rubber ring in its mouth. In December, waves ratcheting up the beach carry the folded bird asleep on the swell, lost in the dark obverse of each rise and fall. And still the lighted headland guards the route to the sea-lanes, although its steading is a mystery. No lighthouse or lightship is marked on the map. And still.

5

The brooks rush into each other wildly, and wildly part, again and again dividing and joining, currents uniting and disagreeing, like a cage of veins, a delta of nerves, capillaries that outrun the mind. Far off, the waters trapped in the Great Central Bog expand in the rising of a dark tide, awakening memories for a few seconds and eclipsing them beyond recall. The four rivers uncoil on their separate journeys: the Barrow sways into the south; the Boyne huddles among passage-tombs; the Shannon mutinies to the last; and the Raven has escaped. There are channels beneath ground running out to the sea, to the deep calm that shatters the storm, expending itself on a black rock far beyond sailor's craft or navigator's skill. We unscrew the telescope, see nothing, and cling to imagination, to the random gesture of each wave, each trick of the dark, anything that seems to re-form itself in space and time, anything trying to grow a shell and survive.

Nature and Costumes

Kiefer's northern landscapes are often winter scenes, zones of natural extinction; but they are also great ploughed fields where, if it survived, anything at all might grow.

1

As the shadows lengthen along hedges and up the small towers of Lombardy, fires are set in a dozen places at once.

Two hares run up a steep field. Even trains cannot get through when the fire bends the iron tracks and fishing canoes swing round in the estuary currents.

2

After dark, the cool green leaves of maize begin to roll and gleam in the breeze.

Under his shirt and over his chest was a fragment of horse chestnut leaf, brown and exhausted before its time.

'I don't do meat, I don't do salt fish, I don't do sweet drinks, I don't do olives, I don't do capers.'

3

The river is dark green in the heat that beats onto stones lined up as irregular stepping places.

The pallid ibis, an unreleased trap, waits in the long irrigation ditch.

Freight trains loaded with the carefully interlaced trunks of poplars, felled nearby, rumble over fresh granite chippings mixed in with grease-soiled debris, ribboned by creeping plants.

The collapsing shells of farm buildings in parcels of meadowland
are entirely walled off by inter-splicing roads and motorway
ramps.

4

Gales rise, and the animals retreat to a disused quarry. They hear
little of distant stirrings and one by one shut down for winter
like the drones in a hive. The tall beeches with erupting bark, the
higher limbs with a dusting of green bacteria, catch pigeons blown
off course.

5

On the banks of the Moldau are filled buds of hazel, weeping
tips of sycamore and the squalling cry of rooks in protest over a
sparrowhawk diving again and again. But a great bird has been
snagged by the weir at Kafka Island, beneath a winter thorn, with
its hard red clots of berry. The tall mast of a dead poplar, with
tetherings of ivy, rises over rough hurdles at field edge, a tower on
the skyline.

Soft yellow corals of lichen appear on the wet beech logs, the
lopped branches of holm oak, the pitched roof with its igloos of
moss.

6

The serial poem advances and retreats. No apparent outrage echoes
inside the great panelled clock case of Our Lady and the English
Martyrs. No blood plasma supplied where none called for.

Lo-st

1

Over a ruined fence, the wire unhasped, the posts half grown-over like graves on the verge of a morth lake, the whistle of a shell.

Life in the dugout, bird-shunned, stale air, dreams of the enemy.

With one foot on the duckboard, at the end of a long trickle of soldiers in mist, mule-corpse, puff-eyed, a meaningless flare.

To step away, feel the peat on Hoy.

2

There are long roads over the bog like causeways over the flats of an estuary. The tide advances and retreats vertically unseen.

The cloud cover is frequently so low as to be on intimate terms with the population. They move in an atmosphere of untrustworthy shapes and volumes, of unfolding lies, floating streamers of disinformation.

3

When partial vision returns, its competence is judged by degrees of clarity in the daily scanning of a territorial marker, such as the horizontal joints in a clapboard shed at the bottom of the garden. This instinctual choice reveals the extent to which defence and ownership have been programmed into the bodily economy, defence first, and ownership second, with a corresponding ratio of urgency and insistence.

4

The cutter, snatching danger from the jaws of safety, takes its cargo
of old guns up the reef-filled channel, the route least expected.
The pounding of the winds, a mimic tattoo of cannon-fire, hurtles
between the flying spray and the rough hoop of horizon barely
glimpsed.

Now the off-shore breakers set hard, the land a mirage.

5

And the whistle is alive and shrill: the traffic policeman's whistle,
the stationmaster's whistle, the referee's whistle. But it also has a
subtle pedigree in the referred whistle: 'O whistle and I'll come to
you', the submissive promise converting into a summons of terror;
'I'd whistle her off and let her down the wind', the coded restraint,
the deceptive permission in a signal of release; 'You know how
to whistle, don't you, Steve? You just put your lips together and
blow', the mouth as mouthpiece and the whistle as tantalus, erotic
when absent.

6

On the journey home, the first class compartment was empty,
apart from a ticket inspector, gloomily filing his nails.

Carmagnole

Not far from the eroded turf and elephant-skinned plane trees
of Southwark Park, the émigré Monseigneur is buried with his
pre-Revolutionary porcelain teeth, glazed and fired at the Sèvres
factory. These are not gnashers but congregation-dazzlers, testy
sermon-performers, biting on sins and improprieties with the
elegant clink of cup against saucer, bone paste and sugar tongs, the
creeping tumbril of decay. Clay blocks the wheels, plastering the
fellies, packed fast, layers of daub. Otherwise it robs the fields and
undoes the work of drills, the seed sown too early.

Gulls rest on warm chimney pots above houses where documents
are shredded and burned. The currents of heated air think
twice about the pinnacles of Southwark Cathedral, churchyard
mortgaged to the railway. Only the bells, pealing blindly, ignore
the ebb and flow of re-routed streets, the metamorphic ripples of
new building.

There is nowhere left that I have not scoured or haunted, not once
or twice but many times. But the place I am most familiar with,
where I am familiar to the casual eye, gliding like a revenant, is the
river with its rotting posts and rusting chains, its drowning shrubs
and choked hedgerow, its deplorable trees.

The first bridge did not go to the opposite shore, but to a gravel
bank in midstream, a reef of the unexplained, proxy for the fourth
dimension. Like the portraits of nudes in which the backbone
loses its way, seems to disappear. These are not studies of anatomy,
but studies in the imagining of being. The artist's book-plate puts
his own hand at dead centre, crooked round an absence, grasping
on air, reaching for brittle shafts of willow stained with mustard
powder lichen; crumbling heads of plantain; dead growth at field's
edge, papery stems of wild chervil, bunches of quaking grass.

The entire landscape is cloaked in parasitical green, ivy drawing
strength from corrupt and dying organisms. It is slowly thinning
out all opposition. Inscriptions on graves are scabbed, deformed,
hidden. The arc of a bramble, reaching across a stack of rusting

girders, each with its spray-painted logo of art-ownership, tightens around the heart of an enemy. Its veto is planted deep in the briar, like a veiled linnet's nest forgotten about.

Paris by Helen

for Marc Atkins

To Repeal the Spoils

They dream continually of enriched uranium.
Only the words are irreplaceable:
fixed languor and tardy dolour.

While you were listening and not paying attention
Ulysses lashed himself to the mist.

Show me your scar again, Ulysses
those volutes and the reappearing
numbness. That was your great discovery

an unreasonable desire for poetry while
swallowing blood. Now you find me shaking something

Penelope's chevril glove, unharmed in the debris
on a worn-out carpet.

Just as the larks lose all sense of their bodies
so you are wearing your skirts much higher

every night in my bed. But my flight of bemusement
will not add up. The occasion demands flight
with its opposite number.

And I am on the verge of a steel vice
with a grief that spares nothing.

If and only if in twenty years time
I have no one else to write for

death will be borrowed and never returned
death will be flitting in the silence.

On the Formation of Splinter Groups

like an imbecile I think I belong to one

where a rope hangs from the tower
I've seen this blindfold before
when words collide or lunge
your lips pass among them
in the aisles of the milking shed
I don't mean it when I say
the torches burn down
on the dying shores of the Caspian
you cannot read by them
but seen in another light
caught by an absent-minded wave
this occurred to me long ago
whoever you are
it must be me writing
this rational séance of consonants
this conflagration of vowels
and digging in the wrong place
all I have ever found
is the formless beauty of the dunes
always embroider the unthinkable
put a face to the voice
come out dead or alive
from the dark galleries
Berlin is a mound of bricks
I imagine you entombed
at the heart of your revolution
a stubborn gate-keeper
all day on the moving staircase
not far from heaven
where there is no consent
crossed by the floating clouds
shirt torn in several places

what do you see in me apart from panic

Fears before Bedtime

this paper does not catch fire
I want the air from your lungs
breathing of what is to come
but the groundswell of opinion
bursts on the present moment
wherever the wind is blowing
let there be an acacia
let there be thistledown floating
past the gun emplacement, beyond
poems that are screwed up, beyond
the net mended for the last time
as slowly as possible
where the sky is upside down and so close
you step from the Gallo-Roman baths
and the tears just come
tears of anger, tears without number
Zazie outside the Métro
is all skin and bone
her little sisters turn out in force
most at home in the open
answering the summons of restless forms
do you want to see the body
rented by the hour
and endlessly rearranged
yes as quickly as possible
dipping your fingers in blood
a little water clears us of
for a few feverish moments
your glance falls to the bottom
of this Sargasso manuscript
thrown in the dustbin
at one stroke we are parted
the ruination of art
a theory of escapology
tightening and loosening the bonds

Assange Militia

I have this feeling for poetry
that it will give away my position.

It is one small step for you and me
one giant leap for librarians,
in sore need of boarding this craft
whose sails can never be trimmed.

We have picked them out of the identity parade
which assembles in silence out of breath;
up and down the artist prowls
wearing the wrong collar size: 'J'accuse!'

What makes you shudder is beyond all measure:
let's start with the froth on this beer, with the disused sickle
and hammer neglected in the attic
where fluff collects. It is mantling the entire earth
long before sunrise. There is just one twinkle
where clouds are drooping, they are reading the instructions
for indoor blood sports.

It has all been thought of before
but nothing is in the right place
and every swerve is fatal
the park gates are closing for good.

The first tendrils of unhappiness are poking through the bars
but something is unlocking somewhere
a something that has been keeping for this.

Let us meet unforeseeably or
never find each other again.

We have heard the waters rising in the Bay of Naples.
We have seen the founding fathers falling in.

Love in Avarice

It was the start of the great fire, we were listing the minutiae
the chair he died in, the trees, the neglected vines
clawing at the window. I could not rid myself of the sounds.
This is the cancelling-out, the striking of the work-house clock.
Resign your place among the mannequins, he said
out of breath in the crowd of lenders. Cut the engine now
and everyone is in step. The scalpel
finds its own way to the core, and its protégé, the tomb
is the rival of his master. We cannot go in the fields
that flash in the rear-view mirror, to the throngs
of the dead drifting apart. They sleep on fetid straw.
The audience is now invisible, the reading committee
suspended, and so we meet again, monsieur molière,
and the leaves drop away like notes
falling from the ATM, in rock-shelter middens.
We were always going to part here
the lullabies that come between us.
Where is it written the train stops dead
in winter dark, because we have eaten our words.
It was the impudence of a moment
to stare you out, brushing away shards.
This is unbreakable glass
and the nearest running water
is far away, bound for a circlet of pines
and the invisible emptiness of the Irish Sea.

Canticle of the Rivets

Take a bolt-cutter to it. She often unravels
the day's warping dream. The old couple dance silently
and carry off the prize. As you talk to yourself
you muster forces. Remove chocks from undercarriage
on the first day of the missile season
the day of wrath, shrouds on the beach. Once you
turn your back on the furthest
outpost, where does it get its funding. They are
hired by the hour, sieving gold, no elbow-room.
A light goes on in the porch and everything
I love is in those fingertips.
In the corridor, the guards are sluggish
in the House of the Epic Poet. They gather round
with palstaves. You speak with another
behind the hangings, waiting for rivets.

Rope-makers all walk backwards to save you
from drowning. Dropping like a stone that has
been hand-picked. And I alone am responsible.
I am alone responsible, gnawing at a loose end
yet again. Wading far out to the whispers
where the scum of language, fish heads, fish tails
collect. You have put all this behind you, but
while the spirit is soaring, the air-raid sirens come to life
and the sea draws back, and nothing can fetter
this longing for wreckage.

Tweeze That

Once you move on from the title and the windfalls
the mirror image is first among equals.
Who is hueing and crying, or sauntering and
slackening pace, always in a gang but never
put out to pasture? Reading over your shoulder
the poem's elliptical orbit, it gave me a start
where I am from. The ink is running in torrents.
And the wrecker's ball is inside me,
it fills the streets with one phrase. All the bulkheads
are smashed aside. It seems to me I have heard that
note on the Atlantic swell, fishing by night.
A new species has been reported
in the blue-green tendrils of jelly-fish.
Will we need steak knives for this?
The words are all fretted and ready:
in the Street of the Lapwing, the name lies in wait
on the tip of my tongue. I am pinning it all
on a light in the ashes, the clinker in the run-off,
and the sand between the toes
of the early morning scavenger,
to whom this belongs.

As the wind moves over to the hop-field
I would not be seen dead in that.

Someone Just Walked Over My

These words are more like objects than a song
with garlic on its breath
                              in unfavourable light.
I feel it on the nape and
thoroughfares of the blood. Language has an expiry date
with light foot, it is the tally-man ignorant of the branch-like
instructions for using your gun-rest. We shall not see its like
the load-bearing syntax of the river
settles everything. Once again
I have reached a dead wall.

The same words are inside you but beating the canvas
where tornadoes roam. Among these fears the
remote playground hubbub. Constantly the horseshoe crab affirms
the hull grinds on the beach like the snake shedding its skin.
I have split my sides at the headland draped in mist.
Where the marsh-bittern haunts, someone just walked over my

poems that need an adaptor, a transformer
with a hard-pressed mother-of-pearl sheen.
Take a squint at the zenith. This is our moon landing moment
end of mandatory speed limit. Come out where I can see you
in the dark hive of the stars. Unless we hear to the contrary

the unalterable dark below stairs.

Translation

Do not read what happens next.
The swifts return without fail
with no room for second thoughts
in no particular language
and we rode all night
on a causeway in the mist.

Do not call it back
from the world to which it clings.
The edelweiss withheld again
the pennant idling in the wind.
That soon wears off
unwriting itself backwards
and the rest is on mute.

To escape down the highway
on two flat tyres
and eat by the light of headlamps
send word, press print
for a time and motion holiday.
The arrow is still in the tree
it is too high up to reach
the bullet is still in the quarry wall.

One Is Not a Number

I have gone into the back yard
lost everything and found

the stairs up to the tower
but time has broken the hasp.
Let's read that again
without the trimmings
I hear a voice telling me
all games have laws that never sleep.
What we behold is censored words that
dance on the back of a painted fan

and I never dared to use it.
A nameless brook is falling into the air
the night waves are crossing the sea until first light

they never told me where she was going
or where her body has its abode. I met
a young boy, he was spooning the sea
into a puddle, so I ransacked the shore for a broken Venice-
glass, anything to help. But then I put it into a drawer
and forgot the words.
                         Now I weigh
myself when half the world is allowed no share
of the remnant of light. When the last of the bees
has gone to its resting place

what shadow lurks on the prairie. I demur on this
I cannot think of an example.

Through a Blow-Pipe

Mother of everything, let me pull myself together.
Zeus! send me another belt and some braces.
This is the only time I have ever imposed more than
one parting kiss on either of you.
Your victory over the heretics is complete.

I keep watch in the time between dog and wolf.
Like Hamlet in arrears, I should like to point out
the drinks deficit. That's one reason for leaving.

But why whisper. In the shadow of this book
I am dispossessed. Wide open stands the door.

I cannot tell a lie, I would love to use only
oil-based sentences, be a man for hire, a poet
for the asking. It is time for another bottle.

While the voice of the people goes on strike
giving way to the drip drip drip
of the lamp with two wicks, casting
two shadows, little by little
all your certainties will be removed.

Looking at the index to this book
and turning towards no one in particular
I can connect nothing with nothing. *Scripta volent.*

There is also the problem of what to put
on the spine—Illy-this or Eeny-that—or
Three Standard Stoppages, another catchy title
when spoken at the top of your voice.
But is a poem kidnapped by its title? In the same
sexy sort of way that Helen was kidnapped
by Paris; or was it Paris by Helen.

The price given is twenty obols
which it says here is seven euros.
On every coin a Gorgon's head.

In my dream we were all entombed in this lukewarm place
with the embers of Parliament still glowing.
But the night-time gangway has been removed.

Night itself has flown—Ovid again slumped outside the gate—
                                                    and someone
approaches, wearing a chiton and tibia-protecting socks.
The Volsci are evidently stirring in the Volscian marches
they want free of the yoke of ISBN tyranny.
In the woods, our half-horse friends are starting a new press
and the winged horses of the Etruscan league hop to it.

A Communication-Cord Touched By the Unknown

I saw the stars drop by Achill Island and the unappeased
northern suburbs burning. There was a sudden build-up of ruins.
Remember when it was the whole armada off course
and chariots at the ready covered with mould.

The hound chasing the stag had already slipped from view
that pulls you down and never lets you go.
Do the animals cooperate or collaborate in this
as they come and go without losing transmission.

I'll give you one refrain and we will finish up
with silence over snow, re-reading an elegy
to the very idea of death. I could bear anything
but at least there was a plot to be harnessed

in those days, and we used up all our breath
dragging this gun carriage through dry fields
straight into the war of names and things.

A Crate of Empties

I remember the electric milk float
leaving everything smashed in its wake

Diary of an Imperial Surgeon

It is always the same time of night, shortly before dawn, when I am called out to attend a new case, usually in one of the far provinces; they present the most trouble. No time is lost preparing to leave, always in the company of two assistants, who rush to enter the door of my consulting room, at the same time, turning sideways to squeeze through it, their backs to one another, never the other way round.

The hours pass quickly on these expeditions, surveying the reports drawn up by officials, usually linguists or political advisors; I find their accounts more helpful than those of medical men, who never refrain from assigning causes to the problem, and proposing the remedy. All I require is an accurate description of symptoms; cartographers are often best at this task.

The arrival is quickly followed by interviews with family members, ready with answers to prepared questions. When were their suspicions first aroused; in what circumstances would the patient slur his speech; who were his most frequent contacts; where did he meet them? The majority of answers are useless, but all are capable of throwing up something valuable, an inadvertent clue to the real nature of the complaint.

The interviews over, the ritual dance is performed, and then we glide into our places, according to strict tradition. My assistants make the first two incisions, one each, in the form of a cross, so that the *orbis terrarum*, the hoop that girds the perimeter of the wound, can be lifted into place. The organs are then removed.

The liver is first: organ of ethnography, recording the history of tribal movements, of folklore and the meanings of consanguinity. In our modern times it has become spongy and incoherent, metamorphic, and careless of its function. It slips through the fingers like a shape-shifter. It no longer discriminates between the raw and cooked, and reeks of the distillery.

The spleen is a mystery, and rightly so. It is a sacred relic entrusted to the body, but can live outside it. If one of the other organs rebels, the spleen sidelines it with a facsimile. In rare cases the spleen is removed altogether, if the advantage gained from these faithful copies is outweighed by its by-product, the massing of non-believers.

The stomach is the body's financial centre. It regulates the flow of imports and exports. It has been a long struggle, but we have taught the body to operate with a unified currency. There have been pockets of resistance, in the subtle guise of hoarding and overspending, hidden enemies of circulation, and many transactions have spread confusion ascribing value to what is patently worthless, and *vice versa*. My case-notes are the property of central planning.

The bowels are the organs of language, the most refined instrument of administration that the body possesses, entitled to the most respect. The bowels transform the world into a conglomerate of policing practices, of permissions and prohibitions, rewards and punishments: the perfect image of empire. The bowels are the key.

The organs are disconnected so that we can re-connect them in the proper order. Over time, they develop new habits or revert to old ones, slipping away from their relative positions. My interventions usually hold good for a generation, but that is long enough for disorder to creep back into the system, for the flows and linkages to reverse and uncouple.

The re-arranging, the choreographing of the organs is the most satisfying part of the procedure. This is when all my tailoring skills are brought into play, bringing back memories of my training at the royal court with imperial tailors. The king's body is the template for the study of anatomy, which is why a sculpture of his noble form is placed in every forum of the empire. And the king's robes are the focus of endless research and innovation. I call them to mind in the moment before I puncture the skin or tissue and throw the first stitch.

Bodies seem to need more stitches these days; more ligatures, more seams, more sutures, more staples, more nuts and bolts. And our fashions in clothing are the outward expression of this seemingly inexorable trend. I have seen men whose garments were more stitches than cloth; more embroidered than woven. The effect is magnificent, but in the long term, it entails more maintenance, more scanning, more health-checks.

And the more stitches and rivets we insert into the fabric of order, the more opportunities we create for unravelling, for dishevelment, for disarray. The organs have begun to tug apart from each other, squandering their resources; they have come to a point where they cannot be patched and darned. Many surgeons have begun to argue that the interviews should be conducted directly with the organs themselves. But the perversity of organs is their desire to speak a different language from everyone else.

It is true, they have mostly forgotten the structures of languages once spoken before empires were formed. Certain items of lexis in these tongues were cognate with the *lingua franca* now ruling. But there are signs on the increase of their trying to retrieve other words, ones that were never cognate at all, and hints of another resolve, to abandon loan words however useful. There is ready assent to the words for universe, taxes, muteness, but each of the organs has its own terms for grain, customs, mutiny. I have seen bodies reduced to ribbons of flesh within weeks of succumbing to this disease.

Yesterday, I passed in the street an old patient of mine rushing in the opposite direction. His clothes were in flitters, his movements jerky, his eyes rolling. And yet there was strange purpose in his agitation—a promise of release in its very lack of coordination— an augury of calmness in all that wildness. As we drew further apart, I was overtaken by a curious, prickling sensation, a feeling of tautness and looseness at one and the same time. As the number of steps between us increased, I imagined a mysterious closeness to this failed experiment, this intimate alien. We were soon lost to one another in the crowd, but secretly we never parted: twins of empire, we turned our backs and faced in different directions, never the other way round.

Klangfarbenmelodie

for Rebecca Horn

The light drops from mimic shower-heads, it burns the skin and exposes the prints of bare feet turning in all directions, unable to fix on one. Then the light goes out.

The bee-hive tomb: a skin peeled away from a dome of metallic light, direct source of lampblack coolness. The domains are aligned, they banish the shades of difference.

Knocking on the wall: dispirited go-devil; pump trolley where no labour is free; the obstinate cradle of strife; a conductress of blue murder.

Its cubic capacity of frets and strings, fingerboards and soundboards, disjected instruments, having no members in common, extorts harmony from passing clouds that raise and lower the temperature of wood, fibre and rosin.

Spinning in time and space, the mirror-planet, where night-insects collide and fall to whispering grass, tumorous mildew, yeasts, and coats of mail through which they grow.

The android dream: music appearing from nowhere; advancing, retreating like Northern Lights in a fourth dimension; no scissoring catgut, players unhinged, a frenzy of pizzicati; only the extragalactic nebulae, coasting in pitted chambers of the brain.

The commander stands, with baton poised, at the open window, ready to conduct the elms and limes, furrowed heathland, wandering country lanes.

All over the building, a series of small reflex hammers is poised, ready to test the deep reactions of its brick, plaster and glass, searching for abnormalities beneath the unexplained behaviour of inmates.

Beyond earshot, in the rubble of an outhouse, a tethered goat is fainting.

Under the observatory roof, disc of the dark, the dust begins to descend. It is borne here on the night air, from a thousand extinguished fires, each one smothered by the vacuum of art, each one kindled by the oxygen of art; the ashes pass through each other, unable to unite.

Will O' the Wisp

In 1942, Adolf Hitler stood on a first floor balcony in Maribor, lampooning the local culture. His immediate audience was a circle of bowed figures, a marble huddle, shouldering the memory of plague. Half-way through his speech with its drench of insults, the sheep-dip of German obloquy, the crowd opened up for a single drunk bearing a large ice-cream cone, overloaded and dripping. Space was needed for the swaying pirouettes of this inebriate, always looping slightly away from his intended course, before pairing up again with his date for the night, his partner in the waltz, the yielding torque of ice-cream. As more and more onlookers turned to smile at this creeping whirligig, the vector of the crowd's attention swung steadily away from the jerking nailbrush moustache of Herr Hitler.

The Führer suddenly realised, in one of his onstage breaks involving a short strut in I'm-a-little-teapot-with-two-handles-mode, that he had been eclipsed, something that had not occurred since the bad old Munich days were succeeded by the good old Munich days. Like thermal imaging, he soon identified the glowing source of this combustion, eyes narrowing in genre-recognition: satire not suicide bomb, character assassin not sniper.

Chaplin, thought Hitler, that little fucker. And his ludicrous film.

The Great Dictator had not been seen in Germany. It had been screened twice for the Party top brass, who all watched it with unnatural restraint, apart from one major who left in the middle of a coughing fit. Chaplin had used his first talkie to strip language of its meanings, filling the screen with street signs in Esperanto and giving his ranting Hitler-figure speech after speech of dyspeptic nonsense. The film contains the last great set-piece of the silent cinema era, a balletic partnership between Hitler and the globe, which is transformed into a gas-filled balloon, spinning and dancing on the fingertips of the dictator who indulges it, teases it and finally destroys it. The disturbing gracefulness of this scene is trounced by the cocky Jewish barber—the second of two parts played by Chaplin—who actually employs the goose-step to kick his boots off before going to sleep in a concentration camp.

But Chaplin was not the inspiration for our Maribor drunk. Unconscious or not, that role belonged to Keaton.

Keaton, mirror for basilisks, whose emblem is a blank tombstone; author of a world whose people misunderstand each other perfectly; where languages outnumber speakers, all silent; married by mistake, employed in error, provided for by accident; loser for whom every door opens, for whom the subway ends in the frozen north, where snow shoes are made out of two guitars; Keaton, who always eludes an army of cops, massing in ever greater numbers; artist of ingenuous ruses; redistributor of chaos; forever in the wrong place at the right time; a conjuror with only one trick: the one where he suddenly finds himself in the other person's shoes.

The Führer-physiology—tightening scalp and bulging peepers—was enough to scramble all the enforcement officers on duty. Guided by ripples in the crowd, they converged at a tilt on the dance not the dancer, flowing around and across the exhibition space, then ebbing to reveal nothing more than a puddle of ice-cream and a pair of emptily standing boots.

Imbeciles. Hitler gathered himself. Boots, he observed, waving aside the hangdog sniffer-gendarmes. Boots, he previewed, that's all that will be left of them.

All that will be left is more than just equipment. All that has been left is a library of boots. Not peasant boots that only sing the song of the earth; not Heideggerean clod-hoppers, stuck-in-the-mud-of-dumb-routine, dignity-of-exhaustion, sweetness-of-anxiety, joy-of-starvation, criminally self-sacrificing, boots; inhabited and owned and barely ever taken off; attached to the silage of only one place; and all in the name of an idiot reliability. These boots are cast-offs, bought in the market second-hand, heels frayed by the city streets, not field-paths: hurrying from the main square in Graz the night the glass was broken; treading rubble in Vienna when Dollfuss ordered in the artillery; following carts and hand-carts along the tow-paths of the Sava above Zagreb; kicking stones in the yards of Szombathely; following at a distance an aloof young woman, limping slightly, in Trieste; migrant boots; revenant boots; boots that have beaten no path, that have not found their way; the seven league boots of the European diaspora; Boot Hill boots; only home of the homeless; shell of the human mollusc; final unresting place; transit-camp where the heart is; ghost hearth for will o' the wisp.

Mayo Mayo

1

Like parch marks on grass, linked in a circle no one alive has seen, pigments arrive, unbidden. Their thermal shadows bleach the matting of roots, the hollows, the infilled tunnels of worm and grub. This chemical starvation assembles a fibrous photographic negative. Just as sculpture is missing space, space now lost to our touch and our breath. But where is the negative of blue, of yellow, of pink: cornflower, hawkweed, moth orchid? Their colouring does not sink down into the page, but rises up out of it.

2

The paper has not had a single drop to drink. The artist has been orbiting his work with the windows closed, but everything outside is in earshot. The blackest bird-shapes have called to him. Only the white stag is frozen in silence at the edge of a field, with something tangled in his crown of antlers. Winter was long, a slow ebb of colour, a rushing flow of silhouettes—organic forms withdrawn into the barrels of microscopes. Let those who live in rented property inherit this: a footprint in sand, the spring in your step.

3

Tip the paper and let the words run. This nacreous sheen that glints once and disappears is the poem coming towards you in an afterimage, long after it has deceased. So where is the poem this minute? On the other side of another universe. There is no window in the earth's atmosphere clear enough to see its form. It comes to you only in fragments, space-debris, the dust on a bird's wing. The creature itself cannot pass between worlds, although its skin and hair become invisible. It has no appreciable size to astronomers, but they wish to clasp it to them.

4

The more movement over the surface, the more awareness of the deep gulfs far beneath. Drawing is like sonar, fetching back the last quiver of sound, the final blink of light, from a retreating source; from the vacuum, always in search of more space and more time, with its furious stillness, its cold, staring impatience. Drawing attracts the trace elements, a cluster of cells, a few strands of warmth, streaks of luminescence in the dark profound. Drawing draws from its hidden source.

5

The sequence of nine drawings, 3 x 3, offers a parallel universe to the poem sequence, which can be read vertically, diagonally, knight's move, hop-scotch. Colours and forms are twinned and tripled in different parts of the grid, joining and parting, elliptically orbiting; sometimes ricocheting among the magnetic fields, they reverse the poles of meaning and intent, become word-welter, confidence trick, or assembly instructions in foreign tongues.

6

The art of drawing, the art of writing, has a dead centre, a black fog that sticks to the lungs, a pain that drags behind perception, but not far enough behind, a dark beacon blazing alone, a discarded torch, still sweating tar, choking the air with burned trash, the kindling of an old fear, of furtive chemical alarm.

On the other bank of the river is a charred mound, the only landmark. It raises questions as dense as pitch, as sluggish as the tides. They pull at the slow, snaking current. The rudderless vessel asks around for a heading. Go not to Lethe, barely rippling, the bow wave soon replies.

Herne

He hunts for a tree no longer there, cut down three times, avoiding the low hills of Bucks and Berks, the canopies of Russian vine, smell of burnt toast, false gables of the express supplies centre. There is a stand of palm trees, vintage graffiti, sales and lettings. There are chairs and tables upended in the long grass, the ticking of the meter, collapsing sewers. Now the bell rings for playtime, this is as far as we get, a procession under dropping masonry. Here come the dark grey hounds and the last light falls on grey tombs, where three men finger worn lettering, tracing their own names.

This obscurity is the fount of invention, a cascade of mockery. But his eyes are failing fast, a billowing dark blue robe floats to the centre of his vision. He has neglected everything, there is a gathering of poets, all with dilated pupils and narrowed irises, let me rest the book in their hands, take it lying down, the pariah dance of trees in a storm, oil on poplar.

Sick to the gills: empty gasholders, cages of air; the past disappears over garden walls, memory chemicals hang by a thread. Herne is the memory of injustice, pest-bearing winds stir up newsprint, witness statements, sycamore leaves have the black spot. Phase one sort bones, human from animal, define cut-marks, name the implements, squalor, ignorance, want, idleness, disease. Phase two re-brand, the fires going out, socialism lodged in crevices, the flashlight of rhetoric mirroring a techno-sublime, dazzling the stake-holders. Phase three the abyss, fragments of mirror in everyone's eyes.

The people lie where they fell, on railway cuttings, heaps of smoking embers. This govt is govt of practical measures, no reverse gear, they delight their eyes with murder pamphlets, statistics of armed men. They tread on the white dust (volumes of white dust pouring through space). Here is a steam shovel and steam covers the sunset. The operator recoils from his panel of dials.

But Herne is also Orion, the blind hunter, marching into the dawn. His guide Cedalion stands on his shoulders, but as they near the edge of the forest, Cedalion looks away, too late. He sees ash, and birds flying through ash, with heavy wings, the felling of the forest, and terrible blast craters. There are poison-crusts and hunger-scratches in the cold earth. He sees lamps flicker and go out, and the return of squalor, ignorance, want, idleness, disease.

But Orion goes forward, feels the warmth of another sun on his face. His retinas hold images of pellucid sky, well-tended fields, men and women waking up, keeping alive the know-how: how to line a well, how to graft the healing plants, how to move a hive, or close a storage jar; how to embank the turning river, or judge the moment for sailing; how to curve a wheel, how to conceal fire, in a fennel-stalk, how to change colour at will, how to enter the mind of a god.

Cedalion tugs Orion to a standstill, his gaze falls on the hanging tree. But Orion tips his head upwards, the images brighten.

Occasional Inuit

Blocked in by ice, the crew of *Erebus* watch. A strange balloon, passing from east to west, climbs and falls on a high current of air. Even the sharpest eye does not detect the length of charred twine in its lee.

This burning fuse, having released a whole flight of slips of paper, carries on in aerial dumb show. The last slip given to the winds was lost to sight weeks before.

The balloon carried nothing but language: denoting provisions left on Beechey Island; or Spring parties, searching by sledge, directed to Jones's Sound and the north shore of Melville Island. The weight of each word in this English passage was heavier than Greenland gneiss.

It provisioned only ideas. Some are strewn in the Barren Grounds, in wastes not seen for a year, printed in reverse on fossil-bearing rocks, their message unvaried, to promise or threaten results that would alternate from reader to reader.

Each word led to a pinpoint in wilderness, to a pixel of time that shrinks in reading, then lengthens to say, 'come back'. But space and time are glacial now. And there is no trace to be found, no reading the caves and arches of ice.

The poetics of fire balloons are reversible. On the recto side, it is 'not one word is wasted'; on the verso, the terrible waste of its four word ballast: '*Read The Other Side*'.

For years, they tried reading the Other Side. They fired off rockets, the balloons flocked over tundra, from Hudson Bay to Alaska. They dispersed their paper credit. But only occasional Inuit picked up the wind-fed rumours, and forwarded them; passing them round and round, turning them over and over.

Prairie Rose

There are no casual bullets in the desert. The only signs of life,
signs of manufacture. This scrapwood drawing instrument is seen
from all angles, a catchpole splint in urban camouflage. Almost
it leaves no shadow, does not call on light to make any decisions
whatever. But where is incendiary evidence of an aim, the smoking
gun of the camera? And what is the difference between pure
and applied garbage? The one fails even to rein in visible surface
debris, the other becomes tethering-post for an entire state. With
or without suction, the extended synonymy of light and power is
terminated here, in a word that jams in the breech, in a bud that
will not blow.

The Cloak

The most affecting stories of urban poverty—workers dying of cold, starving in basements—were penned by a neat bourgeois from a small town whose louvred windows were never opened wide on impulse; its aesthetic awareness was tailored by having to choose the right kind of paving slab, riven or smooth. The repair, maintenance, adornment, beautification of the urban fabric was discussed during evening *passegiate*. The walking and talking was conducted through the main shopping thoroughfare, which itself became the focus for rival schemes of showy benefaction. In this way, the town acquired its world-famous drain covers. Their extravagant designs were meant to publicise the wealth of donors, but only put the lid on their stench.

Over time a faction emerged whose tastes drove them from the city when the hour came to share dreams or voice ambitions. They drifted towards the city walls and walked back and forth on the parapet, pointing out the beauties of the setting sun in its crossing of the mountains. They shunned the stagnant ditches, the culverts and sluggish canals that ran past their own homes, straining to catch a glimpse of far-flung rivers as they dropped to the sea. Before the writer of this story understood he was a writer, he kept company with these river-spotters and mountain-fanciers, praising the great variety of clouds that mantled distant crags as well as the constant mists rising from ancient lakes, until he had become thoroughly acquainted with the Sublime.

He tried the limits of this acquaintanceship through music, which came easily to him. His facility increased with tuition at the state conservatoire, and this took him to the provincial capital. Here all the temptations of the Sublime slowly and surely trickled away. Music swayed him with its harmonies, which brought every yearning for the unbounded within the measure of the human ear. Now the unknown spanned all the wavelengths of human and divine accomplishment. And striking the right note conveniently did not tie him down to specifics.

Nonetheless, the time came very soon for a dramatic change of key. It was during one of his periodic journeys home from the conservatoire that the composer-soon-to-be-a-writer spotted in the distance a man sitting by the dusty road that stretched out of view; as he drew closer, he realised the man was bent double heaving with sorrow. When he asked the matter, the man could not reply but pulled aside his cloak revealing a dead child. In horror, the writer found that he too was unable to speak.

When he understood that he was hearing nothing: nothing falling from the poor man's lips; nothing from his own lips; nothing even from his own mind; the writer began to wonder about the quality of this nothing. The harmonies that had formed in the air around his every pulse of feeling—like clouds spinning themselves from the collision of warm and cool breezes—simply vanished. Music had been sucked into a void, with nothing to take its place.

Into this deadened world came the smallest flicker of life, like the flare of a match inside a blackened dome. It was the poor man's voice, feeling its way in the dark towards the gossamer-like trance of words leading him almost against his will towards failing light. He began to tell his story—for the first and last time, since in the act of listening the writer could not help changing words, adding several details while leaving many out; and in general making the story his own; and the poor man perfectly realised this before laying his burden down.

By the time he had finished listening, the writer knew what to say; about the man's departure with his wife and child from the town in which they had starved; about their begging along the roads and canals with nothing to eat but dried acorns; about the time when man and child had grown so weak that the wife left them to ask the stevedores working the canals for food to last them to the provincial capital—but she had been gone a long time and the man doubted what had happened to her. He was bound to remain in case she should ever return, but meanwhile the child's body had become corrupt, and the man understood she had slipped away. All that might be preserved was the memory of their flight; and the poor man could now relinquish this charge to his listener.

'But in order to render your own account,' he told the writer, 'you must clothe it in the form of this child,' and he tore away half the cloak he was wearing to wrap around the body. 'Take her back to the town and bury her body in the garden of the highest tower. For there is the grave that is nearest to heaven.'

And this the writer did, scarcely believing his own actions. Years later a great oak tree grew, arching its boughs to cover the whole tower, and it became the highest point among the proud battlements, cupolas and pinnacles of the town.

But from down in the street, to those who crouched along the gutters, the boughs of the tree resembled the arms of a child, stretching up to the clouds as they sailed over earth and into the night. While to those with leisure to climb the tower, pausing now and then for the views to be had from airy galleries, there was time to choose a different form of words; and for them the enveloping oak resembled nothing so much as a great, spreading cloak, extending its shadow over the town and hiding all its imperfections.

Turned to Tongue

Most of those mentioned here are already dead. But their words are still heard in the corridors of the Palace, in the retiring-rooms, in the great Hall. So much happened in the flash of a single moment—before even the writer has had time to think. Now everything depends on committing the act to memory in one of the concealed places of the mind.

I am forbidden to write and speak in my own tongue, which means that none of these arrows will hit the target. When you step aside from your chains, you have lost hold of their true meaning. And this is ministering to your own downfall.

I have dreamed in one hour of so many ways to stage the tragedy. Under this leafless tree, a net is spread before a vast expanse of water. On the horizon, a long plume of smoke never ceases to rise. The use of perspective is to deceive the eye, as everyone knows—just when the other senses are trying to awaken.

Why in a garden full of fruits, do we refrain from tasting any? When we close all the passages to sense and slip into deepest sleep, they collapse and spill forth the urges within them.

According to Signor Castiglione, 'common labourers in the field working under the burning sun will often relieve their tedium with simple country songs. And the ordinary peasant girl, rising before dawn to spin or weave, uses music to ward off sleep and make her work agreeable.' But aren't these songs cries of anguish in the dark, imaginary disembodiments for those who eat nothing but raw herbs?

The words are carried from one place to another, like articles of trade, and are always cheapened. When I cast up my life, longing to bring back the tinder and steel of beauty and grace that set me on fire—and put them down in writing—I can barely endure to return to this wintry employment, to this long civil twilight. It is like teaching a bird to return to its cage. And the depredations go on.

There was one who sought to enlarge our desires when it was against reason to do so. His plan misfired, and the soldiers came for him in the night. Light was beginning to shine through the clefts in the rocks when he and his wife drank poison prepared for them. They went to their room without torches. As the venom took hold of the veins, their words froze in the air. Afterwards, the soldiers took his tongue out and fed it to the dogs, but they are both still spoken of; in the city of light in the republic of air, in the court of miracles.

The Commission

Paid for by a Knight of St John, Caravaggio's *St Jerome* was first transmitted onto canvas in Malta, remaining there ever since. The Knights clung to the island for nearly three hundred years as sea traffic controllers: their purpose to stop the pilgrim ships vanishing off the radar. The geography and history of the Christian world registered as persistent blips until yesterday; and even now, they roll across the screen subliminally as ghost ships.

Everything was balanced on the pivot of the Knights' limpet-shell endurance, just as the orbit of holy scripture round the earth— above the mottled skin of continents, glittering seas, cloud-racks— was encompassed by the heel of Jerome's writing hand.

Caravaggio's Jerome has almost undressed, without noticing— from sheer concentration. Or: he has sloughed the trademark red robes to expose the body of the sitter, which was that of an aging man inured to physical labour. The well-shaped white torso, the sunburned head and hands, look like they came from the nearest boat. They do not take kindly to acts of writing. The hands belong to a fisher of fish, heaving on his nets, not to a fisher of men, alighting on his words. They encase the inkpot as if it would break; they nurse the pen as if it would fly away.

Jerome did not scry the history slipping aside from the pen's advance and coiling and churning like the wake of a slaver's galley; mingling the ink of hope with all blood-types. But for hours he would chain his mind to the task.

The sitter had never learned the correct movement of fingers; or how to push the quill to begin its seismic dance. For him, the roll of vellum was a dead calm, a wide gulf where mind would not stir; where landfall was not even the brush-filament of an idea.

A Turn around Agnès Thurnauer

1

One day the artist released a bird in her studio. It was never seen again but the idea of a bird settled in every painting before taking flight to the next. The task was to paint the sound of its wings.

We can paint an idea of invisible worlds; or leave a single planet in the lurch.

No brush is like another. A poem has the bloom of a moment; every moment is shackled to its DNA: the moment when a flock of starlings tacks to the side, plunges to earth, puts its head in the clouds.

Your painting unseats me—all I can do is climb back in the saddle of poetics, keep going, face up to what the two hold in common, take my pulse, read your lips.

If an artist is born with each work written or painted, what they are selling is worth nothing. When theory comes before the work, this is the new obsolescence. Leave your theory in the garage and walk up the hill. Do not theorise, but outwit.

The end has stolen a march on the beginning. Here, painting lies fallow, waiting; waiting to germinate; breathing in, breathing out; hugging its own limits, like a field-edge path cleared in haste.

Those brakes where we saw the white stag are closed up on the painting's surface. They lead to one level only of the visible, where light and dark have come to an agreement.

The poet lies down on his litter of words and is carried away.

In a painting, before and after exist on the same plane. It can take your breath away, the retinal effect of even the lowest tier. Enough to put the old guard on guard, to raise their shields.

Painting is all the result of acts of destruction: eliminating the uproarious light; seeking to dislodge those entrails folded up in the everyday.

This idea has dropped anchor.

This idea has been carried along by the currents of the stream.

This idea is not cornering very well, the tread has worn off the tyres.

There are traces of oil paint on the steering wheel.

3

Painting engluts the poem—which has no choice in the matter. But the painting clouds over suddenly, suddenly announcing the deluge. You can part the waves only with a voice or a brush.

It is only in flight that bodies take on true form. But the spirit is not always present when the body makes its moves. (It is still coming for us.)

Forget everything you have read up till now. I have taken paintings from the walls of all the museums of Europe and re-routed them, as a peace-offering to my dialogue coach.

This is not the way I absent myself from the text. The text is only an implement, the implement like a miraculous draught of fishes, with me as bait: the better to be digested, absorbed and running through the veins of a reader; reading come what may.

All boats need a prow; no prow needs a figurehead. The ship of state is not a punt.

In the face of such images, we can only curl up to protect ourselves; even the painter must be sedated when painting comes into its own.

But this painting takes me under its wing, trying to smooth away the fault-lines in which we live—like this hand moving against the small of your back.

In the background of the painting, all the words are out of their sockets, to make the eyes get in tune with the ears.

We part company at the top of the hill without looking back: in all directions, the slight inclination of despair.

I have all the good manners I need to get rid of. (At least one before this night is out.)

What is the address of this poem.

What is the direction of its flow.

What is the postcode of the interlocutor.

What is the who gives a flying fuck.

My wings are beginning to leave me.

5

The work-time of the poem slips through the fingers and runs down to the sea that murmurs in all languages that rhyme and recur.

The work-space of the poem is more restricted, but its abbreviations can fill a tennis court with song and all through the stirring of tiny hairs.

Spiders have been at work to repair their nets that mock ours. The scene is set for the painter to announce the Bill of Rights.

Ear-splitting events need paintings.

The maker loves his art, but must the art love its maker? This is the stuff that tutus are made of: mimic intimacy, hollow music.

The painting speaks of little beyond the studio wall; the poem beats at its own words. All territory annexed is the floating island Incognito.

Only one painting at a time is heard clearing its throat.

6

These silent staring forms outlive my capsules and injections. I withdraw all medication, count backwards, prick the blister of compromise.

This bridge in the air between vessels that do not communicate says that they do.

Led onward by your gaze, they cry, Retire. Retire from the arena. I have worked myself loose like giant's robes upon a minor celebrity. I am no longer part of the pressed flesh.

Nothing stirs or sends forth a light, when consciousness returns.

In the absence of humming.

There is a smell of wood shavings.

The sound of footsteps.

A galaxy going out.

First necessity is caparisoned with a name and summoned to the cave.

Art is the last man standing still wearing his sorority patch. He must have shivered at every step. Tamed by what is wild, he acquired a taste for mothering.

Do not give this a date. Assign no dates. Time moves by capillary action, from the centre to the edge. The maddening endless contemporary is always untimely.

I brood over dead things disgorged from the belly of the painting which this book then carts around.

With painting staring straight at us, saying love me, love my fork supper, we turn to art as we turn to resume a conversation.

Step away now.

Light enters the painting and the painter seals up the entrance. Amid the market's razzle-dazzle, we need obscurity.

Time levels all the ramparts we raise against it, and the invisible dust of monuments turns around the artist continually. She unlearns everything.

Even in the thickest layers of paint there are gaps, holes, emptiness, nothing, giving us the unimpossibility of painting.

These gaps compose now the soundtrack of the future. We are too far downstream to be able to return.

Some measure their distance from the bank in the echoes of their words. Others navigate by sight alone, drawn into the high depths of a convex mirror.

Once you begin a text, it is never finished.

Storm Songs

1

I am going to be a diver-swallow
and prove my mettle. The nest is
glued to the eaves where the Odra flows
past the car park, the whispering limes,
and the confines of ice melting atop
doggers and stag-party survivors
bowed down by excessive weight of
chemical antlers. The terminal needle unsheathed
at the end of each verse
came from nothing. These without hope
came from nothing
for the third and last time
bells ring on islands splitting the water
with its own mouthpiece of osier and willow.
Pointless birds whistle or rustle
and Spring creeps in with a loaded gun
from the blood garden of childhood.
A shot rings out and is happening
far into the moss of the night.
The water-rail trembles on the bank
its open beak rolls aside
with the false semitones of a
departed child. The moon lights up
the rest in the gliding of an instant.
Over the hills and far away
the infirmary of memories. The neighbouring hamlets
were not Barking. And you
little black circles round the eyes of morning
as it first appears to the paupers of the forest
I was once like you, Slavonic and unknown.

Let me bisect one of the Alps
and consider white light in those alleys
far beneath lakes others have dreamed of.
Ideas collide in a Muse-box
words go to form clouds
and the dead volcanoes shall say
they were forced to look on her shoulder-blades.
They saw your gaze in her eyes.
There were lilies and frog-spawn
in equal measure, some neat wild pansies
and a sudden wormcast of news.
You put your moist ear to the ground
but neither man nor mountain moved
and ineffable thought sank into
impenetrable brain: the brain
of the New Polish Countrywoman.
She was dreaming awhile of a science
being noisily sick of these harmonies.
And further description would have to include
her lightning-long grief at the death
of her dog (called Nightingale) which
strayed right onto the field of battle
to relieve itself. Giotto didn't *pinxit*.
And there isn't a touch of Dante
in the description of her abandonment
at the wheel of her car.
There is nothing of Plato in her 4 x 4.

3

I sat me down by the waters of
nowhere that's any concern of yours
and asked them to graft some sense onto
the echoes that dogged me, leaning over
my own reflection to loudly insist
'What, I ask you, can poetry do
to arouse the angel of melancholy?'
but my foot slipped on the slipway
and everything remained unsaid.
So the ebb and the flood did not reply
'You mad thing you. I used to think
there were voices that came round
every few centuries, just like a comet
to scorch the snakes among the ruins
and stop up the spring from flowing along
between counter-feeling and counter-reason.
Warsaw is strangely bright tonight
and that reminds me that contradiction
must always abut on the Vistula poplars.
Yet that particular current is now
no more than one long streak of piss
singing comfortably to itself.' 'I know nothing,' I said
'about comets; but it seems to me that some of
these starfish that do not speak
are burning to have their tongues set loose
in the storm that is coming behind that hill.'
'You, whom history calls ERA,' said the waters
'you cannot grasp what unformed words
will show you the grave of the anthropocene.'
We talked a bit more about things angelic
(or rather we didn't, because none of this happened)
but were never alone; and when two men approached
with two great mastiffs to stage a fight
at the water's edge, the flood receded in a ruby glow.

Come out if you will excuse my saying so
We have got you surrounded.
From the west, with mendacity.
From the south, with despondency.
From the north, with very few enticements.
From the east, where perdition brightens.
In the valley of Roncevalles
where the ear still catches
the songs of Omniscience to Immensity
you resemble herdsmen by their fires
like silly moths, who have gathered to develop
the question of silence
enforced by the veto
that is constant noise.

All flowers remind me now of the grave
and the smell of snow the obstinate beauty
of coffin-larch. How far will it spread.
There is a place in the heart, a refugee camp
and the shining women are standing there
eyes dark and deeply set.

They came to a place with a dynamo
no birds had taken flight
and he held a shoemaker's awl
to hack the sentences out.

I reproach myself for this referential
when ancient forms are accounted trash
and the last word choked out of them
puts on a hideous mask.

There is no room for exceptions
when it says that I should not write
we have fought with beasts at Ephesus
too late to put anything right.

Acknowledgements

'Batavia', in *Critical Quarterly*, vol. 45, no. 3 (Autumn 2003).

'Terra Infirma', in *The Literary Review: an international journal of contemporary writing* (Winter 2005) vol. 48, no. 2.

'9/11, Santiago', in *The Liberal*, (February/March, 2005).

'Lady with Vermin', in *These Pages Are Marked By Women: Anthology of the Contemporary Women's Poetry Festival 2006*, ed. Emily Critchley and Neil Pattison.

'The Westralipede', 'Delivering the Device', 'After Archilochus', in Rod Mengham, *Diving Tower* (Equipage, 2006).

'Five Year Plan in Four Years' / 'Plan quinquennal en quatre ans' [translation by Philippe Demeron], in *Les Citadelles: revue de poésie*, no. 14 (Paris, 2009).

'The Debauchery of Nuances', in *Cambridge Literary Review*, vol.1, no.1 (Michaelmas, 2009).

'Bend the Bow', in *Cambridge Literary Review*, vol.1, no.2 (Lent 2010).

'Five Portraits', in *Les Citadelles: revue de poésie*, no. 15 (Paris, 2010).

'Engineering Works', 'Ad Nauseam', 'Repeat This', in *Veer About* (*Veer*, no. 37), ed. Adrian Clarke and William Rowe (London: 2011).

'Nature and Costumes', in *Blackbox Manifold*, no. 6 (March, 2011): www.manifold.group.shef.ac.uk

'Coal Train Still Life' and 'Suffixes', in *The Second Annual Sussex Poetry Festival Magazine*, ed. Laura Gadsden and Joe Luna (Brighton: 2011).

'Icarus Alight', in *Les Citadelles: revue de poésie*, no. 17 (Paris, 2012).

'To Repeal the Spoils', in *Island*, no. 130 (Tasmania, 2012).

'Diary of an Imperial Surgeon', in *The Warwick Review*, vol. VII, no. 2 (June, 2013).

'Assange Militia', 'On the Formation of Splinter Groups', 'Canticle of the Rivets', 'Tweeze That', 'Someone Just Walked Over My', 'Love in Avarice', in *PN Review 215*, vol. 40, no. 3 (January–February, 2014).

'Klangfarbenmelodie', 'Will o' the Wisp', 'Mayo Mayo', 'Herne', in Rod Mengham, *The Understory* (Edinburgh: Corrupt Press, 2014).

'Fears Before Bedtime', 'Translation', 'One is not a Number', 'Through a

Blow-Pipe', 'A Communication-Cord Touched by the Unknown', 'A Crate of Empties', in *Paris by Helen* (Old Hunstanton: Oystercatcher Press, 2014).

'Prairie Rose', in *Visual Verse*, vol. 1 (April, 2014): www.visual-verse.org

'Occasional Inuit', in 'The Polar Muse' supplement, *PN Review 220* (November–December, 2014).

'The Commission', in *outLINES: From the Small Press* (University of Westminster, 2015).

'The Cloak' and 'Turned to Tongue', in *PN Review 222* (March–April, 2015).

The author wishes to thank the editors of all these journals and also John Kinsella, Dylan Harris and Peter Hughes, the editors of Wide Range Chapbooks, Corrupt Press and Oystercatcher Press, respectively.